FLAT or ROUND?
EARLY DISCOVERIES ABOUT OUR PLANET

by Margot Shales
illustrated by A. J. Garces

Chapters

The Flat Earth 4
Chasing Shadows 6
Scoping Out the Planets 10
Believing Is Seeing 16

Harcourt

Orlando   Boston   Dallas   Chicago   San Diego

Visit *The Learning Site!*
www.harcourtschool.com

Nowadays, if you want to know something about the world around you, you need go no farther than your computer. By searching the Internet, you can find the answer to just about any factual question you may have. If you type "circumference of the Earth" into a search engine, you're sure to find a site or two that can point you to the answer.

Of course, before we had the convenience of the Internet (or of librarians, who are the best search engines in the world), people had to figure out other ways to find out about the world. Many facts that we take for granted today were discovered hundreds or even thousands of years ago. Early discoverers could not enroll in classes taught by expert scientists. Instead, they depended on their own observations.

For example, consider what we know about the solar system and the planets. Long before we had satellites in orbit sending us pictures of the universe, we knew a great deal about our neighborhood, the solar system. Early discoverers weren't cosmonauts or astronauts floating in space, consulting altimeters and working out complicated formulas. Those who lived before our modern era could only observe and then think creatively about what they saw. These activities were more than enough to lead the early discoverers to scientific breakthroughs, because observation and imagination are at the root of all science.

The Flat Earth

Everyone knows that Christopher Columbus was one of the few people of his time who believed that the Earth was round, right? As the story goes, in the late 1400s, Columbus wanted to sail west to reach China and he disregarded those who warned him that he would sail off the edge of the world. However, this oft-repeated story is not true. By Columbus's time, most people knew the Earth was round.

The first person on record to note that the Earth was probably a sphere was the Greek philosopher Aristotle (384–322 B.C.). Aristotle figured it out without satellites or telescopes, simply by looking in a new way at an eclipse of the moon.

Aristotle guessed that an eclipse of the moon was caused by the shadow of the Earth. The Earth comes between the sun and the moon, and the shadow of the Earth crosses the moon. Aristotle saw that the shadow was curved.

What Aristotle Could See

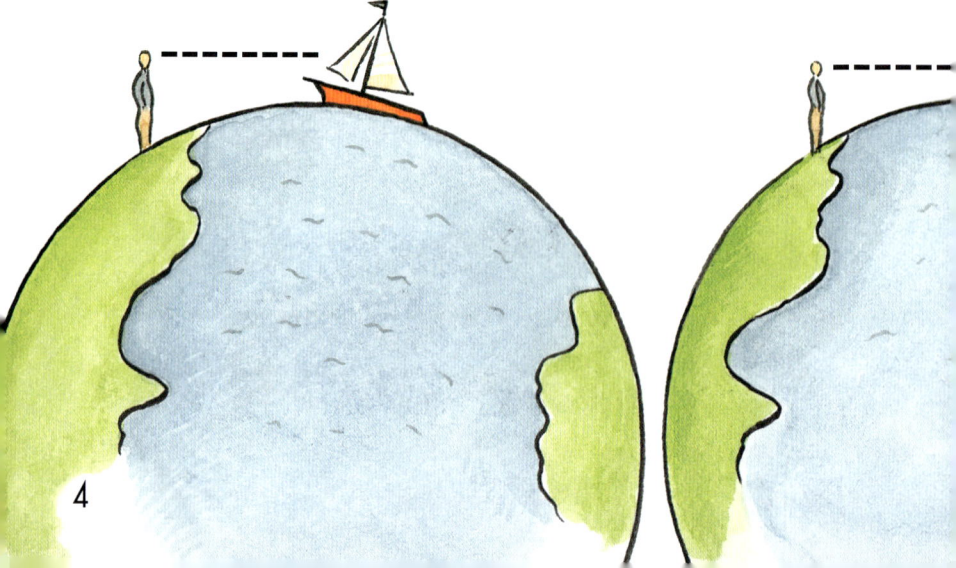

That observation alone proved only that the Earth was circular (like a dime), not that it was a sphere. Yet Aristotle had observed something else that led him to believe that the Earth was a sphere. He'd watched boats sail away from Greece and vanish over the horizon. He'd noticed that when a ship sailed over the horizon, it didn't just disappear; instead, it disappeared in stages.

These two things—the way a ship disappears over the horizon, and the shadow of the Earth on the moon—led Aristotle to declare that the Earth was a sphere. By the time Columbus came along nearly 2,000 years later, most educated people thought Aristotle was right. His observations made sense to them.

Then why didn't anybody try to sail around the world before Columbus? The answer is that people thought the ocean was too large to cross. Columbus simply believed it was smaller than everyone said; his discovery of the Americas was a lucky accident.

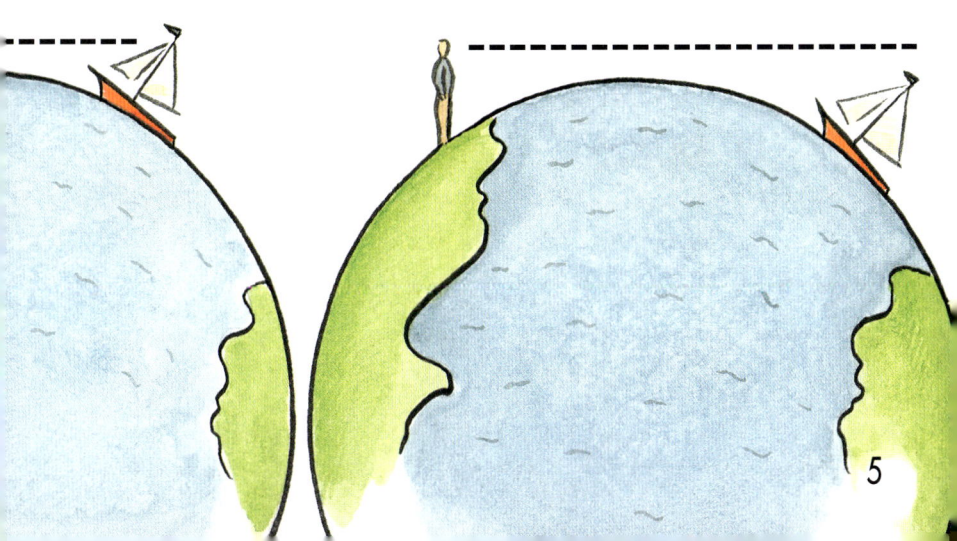

Chasing Shadows

The earliest person to come up with a somewhat accurate idea of the Earth's size was a Greek man named Eratosthenes (276–194 B.C.), whose work in Greece and Egypt as a librarian, mathematician, and geographer make him one of history's greatest minds. Eratosthenes figured out the distance from the Earth to the sun as well as the size of the Earth—thanks to a little geometry and (once again) shadows.

Eratosthenes had read about a town named Syene, in what is now Egypt. There, once a year—on June 21—the sun cast no shadow in a deep well but instead shone straight down to the pool of water at the bottom. Eratosthenes realized that this phenomenon meant that in Syene the sun was directly overhead once a year.

In other words, if one drew an imaginary line from the town to the sun, the line would be perfectly straight and perpendicular to the town. Some people might say "So what?" but Eratosthenes knew a lot about geometry (and therefore about triangles), and he thought of a little experiment he could do.

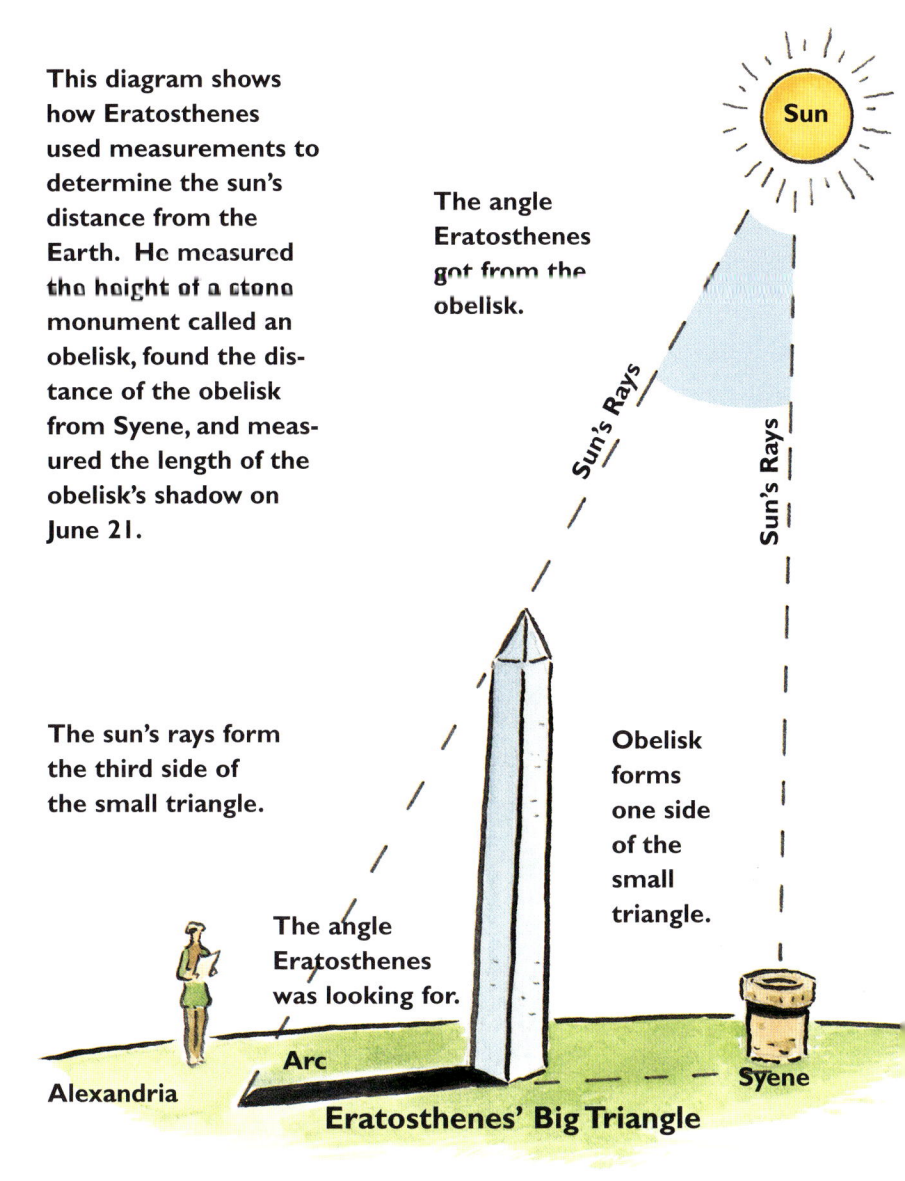

This diagram shows how Eratosthenes used measurements to determine the sun's distance from the Earth. He measured the height of a stone monument called an obelisk, found the distance of the obelisk from Syene, and measured the length of the obelisk's shadow on June 21.

The angle Eratosthenes got from the obelisk.

Sun

Sun's Rays

Sun's Rays

The sun's rays form the third side of the small triangle.

Obelisk forms one side of the small triangle.

The angle Eratosthenes was looking for.

Alexandria

Arc

Syene

Eratosthenes' Big Triangle

Eratosthenes' Little Triangle Shadow forms the base of the small triangle.

7

As it turned out, Eratosthenes did not come up with a completely accurate calculation of the Earth's distance from the sun, although the number he did come up with was off by only a small percentage. The figure must have shocked him. The sun is 93 million miles away from the Earth, an unimaginable distance for the people of Eratosthenes' time. It must have been difficult for Eratosthenes to convince his peers that his calculations were correct.

In any case, once he had a rough idea of how far away the sun was, Eratosthenes could use this information to get an idea of how big the Earth was. Again, he used geometry.

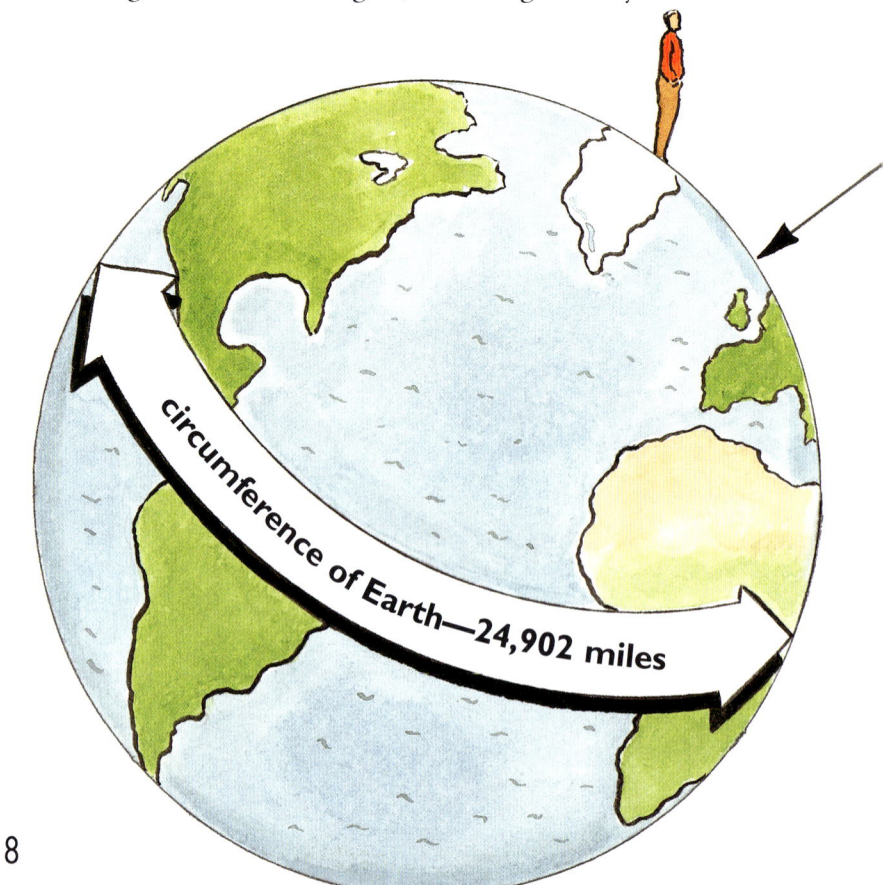

circumference of Earth—24,902 miles

distance from sun
93 million miles

Eratosthenes knew that Syene was about 500 miles from Alexandria. Using his other calculations, he knew he could determine how big a piece of the Earth's circumference (the distance around the center) that 500-mile distance represented. In fact, it was an easy matter for him to figure everything out. He calculated that the Earth's circumference was 24,662 miles.

In the end, Eratosthenes was off by about 240 miles; the Earth actually measures 24,902 miles around. However, his figures were very close for someone who used nothing but shadows and a pencil.

Imagine the sorts of things Eratosthenes might have calculated if he had had a telescope; he might even have figured out that the Earth orbits the sun instead of the other way around—but that discovery would not be made for several centuries.

Scoping Out the Planets

In the early 17th century, the Italian scientist Galileo Galilei (1564–1642) heard about a fabulous device called an *optick tube,* which the Dutch had invented. This device could make faraway things look large. After Galileo heard a traveler describing the device (a long tube with two glass lenses), he immediately went home to make one for himself. The device (later called a telescope) had been around for a few years by this time, but the Dutch were using it as little more than a toy—to spy on people across a crowded square, for instance.

Galileo saw the potential the device had for defense—with a telescope, a city could see armies approaching long before the armies saw the city—so he demonstrated the telescope for the city noblemen in Venice. Galileo also had the idea of pointing the telescope at the night sky. People had pondered the stars for eons; finally a device had been invented that could bring the viewer closer to those distant objects.

Telescopes are simple to fashion from two kinds of lenses. The first lens is a magnifying glass, also known as a convex lens (meaning the glass is fatter in the middle than at the edges). Magnifying glasses make objects look larger but distorted. These lenses had been used for centuries before telescopes were invented, to help aging scholars with weak eyesight read manuscripts.

The second kind of glass necessary in a telescope is a concave lens (meaning the glass is thinner in the center and fatter toward the edges). This lens puts close-up things in sharp focus but makes them look more distant. To create a basic telescope, one need only hold the concave lens close to the eye and the convex lens at arm's length.

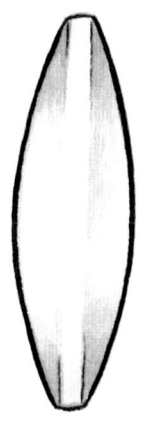

Convex lens

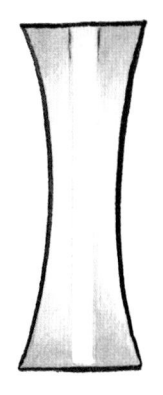

Concave lens

11

The very first telescope Galileo constructed made things appear three times closer and nine times larger than they appeared to the naked eye. Soon, however, he made a telescope that enlarged objects more than sixty times.

The first celestial object at which Galileo aimed his improved telescope was the moon. As he watched shadows stretch and squish across its surface, he realized that the moon glowed with reflected sunlight and, further, that it had mountains and valleys similar to the Earth's.

Galileo published his observations in a book, and though he didn't know it yet, his suggestion that the moon and the Earth were similar was the beginning of serious trouble for him. Leaders of the church of his time didn't like what they read in Galileo's book, but Galileo was too busy to listen; he had his eye glued to his miraculous telescope.

Galileo directed his gaze to the stars, discovering that many constellations had more stars than anyone had known. To the naked eye, the Pleiades appear to consist of six or seven stars. With his telescope, Galileo counted several dozen. The sky, he realized, is much larger than anyone had dreamed.

Something else Galileo observed was the planet Jupiter. Over the course of two or three years, Galileo mapped the motion of tiny bodies around the great planet. He came to realize that the Earth was not unique in having a moon. That idea led him to believe that he was viewing a miniature planetary system, not unlike that of the sun and the Earth and the other planets. Those two ideas led him to realize that the Polish-born astronomer Nicolaus Copernicus (1473–1543) had been correct in suggesting that the Earth and the planets orbited the sun.

This idea sounds like an obvious truth now, but in the time of Copernicus and Galileo, the church taught that the Earth was the center of the universe and that everything else orbited it. Indeed, one didn't need to look far to find confirmation of this church doctrine: Did the sun not trace its orbit each day by rising in the east, moving through the sky, and setting in the west? To say otherwise was to risk persecution, excommunication, or worse by the church.

Galileo, who never listened to his friends when they urged caution, felt secure from being punished by the church, so in a book he published in 1632, he declared that the Earth orbited the sun. Galileo was put on trial for what he had claimed in his book. Threatened with serious punishment, he refuted everything he had observed and written about.

Galileo professed to agree with the church that the Earth was the center of the universe. He swore that he would never again speak or write in support of the Copernican theory, and he told the court that he had been mistaken—that in fact, the Earth did not circle around the sun along an orbit like the moon around the Earth and, furthermore, that the Earth did not move at all. How difficult it must have been for Galileo to pretend that what he knew to be true was not true at all.

However, prideful Galileo may have gotten in the last word, anyway. Legend has it that just before he was led away from court, Galileo dejectedly scuffed his toe against the floor and muttered, "And yet it does."

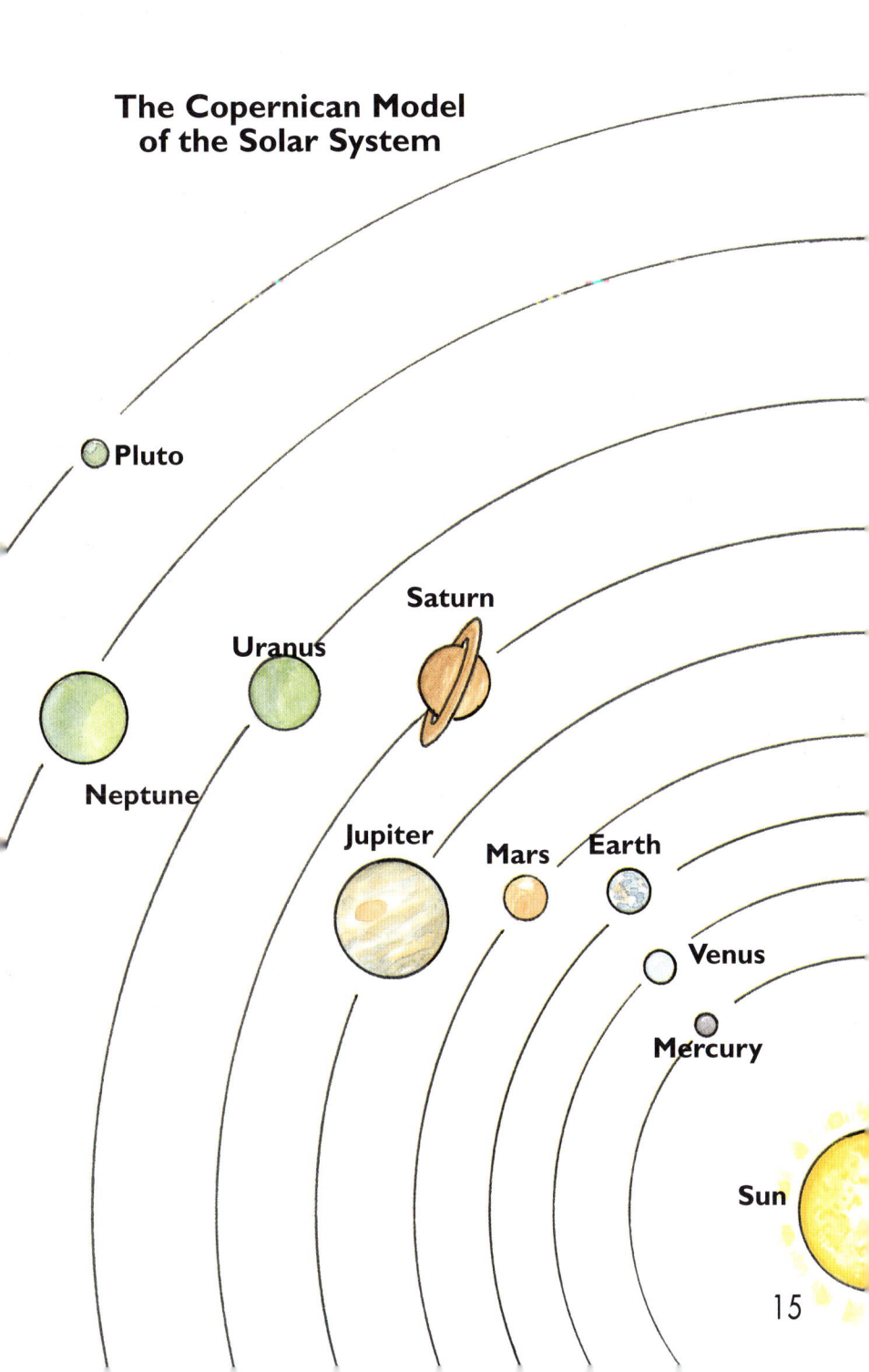

The Copernican Model of the Solar System

Believing Is Seeing

Even though Galileo recanted his claims, the church could no longer promote beliefs about the world that people could see for themselves were wrong. Though the church banned the books written by Copernicus and Galileo, copies still circulated, and those with scientific minds used their eyes and their imaginations to confirm what Galileo and Copernicus had seen.

These new astronomers were not about to allow church beliefs to dictate what they saw. Instead, they trusted their mind's eye—that visionary place where analysis and speculation work together to solve the puzzles presented by the world. In doing so, they were falling back on the first two tools of a scientist, the same that led Copernicus and Galileo to make their assertions: keen observation and an open, questioning mind.